DUNCAN CAMPBELL

CONTENTS

FOREWORD

This survey of Duncan Campbell's inventive and provocative practice looks back over the steadily accumulating line of arresting, meticulously assembled film works that this Dublin-born, Glasgow-based artist has produced during the last decade, and coincides with the launch of the latest in that series, *Make it new John* (2009). Commissioned by Film and Video Umbrella, Tramway, Chisenhale Gallery and The Model, Sligo, this 50-minute hybrid of documentary, fiction and essay-film exhibits many of the signature motifs and preoccupations that have distinguished Campbell's work to date – not least in its fluent and resourceful marshalling of disparate archive material, and in its equally deft and insightful appraisal of recent social and cultural history. Ostensibly a study of the life and times of the maverick motor manufacturer John DeLorean, *Make it new John* is also a freewheeling tour of post-war American iconography, invoking the universal American dream of freedom of mobility (and an equally prevalent urge to 'start over') while reflecting how these desires have found increasing expression in the accelerated turnover of consumer products, especially cars. One such manifestation of America's love affair with the automobile, and a prototype for a new-model 'car of the future', was the distinctive DMC12 sports car that popularly established, and eventually tarnished, DeLorean's name. Using a mix of contemporary footage and after-the-fact reconstruction, *Make it new John* examines DeLorean's frustrated efforts to mass-produce this now-iconic vehicle in the uncertain economic and political environment of Belfast in the late 1970s/early 1980s and traces the personal fall-out of that failed endeavour.

Illustrated by stills from the film, and through supplementary material uncovered in Campbell's researches into the subject, this complex story is further elaborated, over the pages of this publication, in two newly-commissioned texts which extend their compass to Campbell's body of work as a whole, highlighting earlier stand-out pieces, such as *Falls Burns Malone Fiddles* (2003) and *Bernadette* (2008), whose aesthetic properties and polemical ambitions anticipate and inform the new film. On behalf of everyone at Film and Video Umbrella and Tramway, we would like to express our gratitude to Martin Herbert and Melissa Gronlund for their perceptive contributions, and to everyone else who has played a part in realising this book – in particular to Arts Council England and Scottish Arts Council for their generous financial support. Our thanks go also to The Model, Sligo for partnering us in this initiative and to Chisenhale Gallery, whose co-commissioning of *Make it new John* was crucial in instigating this wider collaboration. Finally, though, our special thanks go to Duncan Campbell, whose energy, commitment and imagination have made this such an enjoyable project.

STEVEN BODE, Film and Video Umbrella
SARAH MUNRO, Tramway

A VOICE, NOT YOUR OWN

Following the huge box-office success of *Back to the Future* in 1985, John DeLorean wrote a letter to Bob Gale. According to the recipient, it read, in part, 'Thank you for keeping my dream alive.' Gale was the producer of that Hollywood film, a vehicle for Michael J. Fox. DeLorean was the creator of the iconic, gull-winged DMC12 sports car that was used as Emmett 'Doc' Brown's time machine in the movie, but which by the mid-'80s wasn't really a vehicle for anybody. Three years earlier, the DeLorean (as it is widely known, being the only vehicle produced by the short-lived DeLorean Motor Company), had ceased production after just 9,000 cars had rolled off the assembly line at the DMC factory in Dunmurry, Northern Ireland. The car is a vexed and paradoxical symbol, at once desirable – mostly, as its architect acknowledged, thanks to a teen comedy made when the DeLorean was unavailable – and an index of failure.

In 2007, two years after John DeLorean's death, it was announced that DMC was back in business and would be building DeLoreans again, due to popular demand. The proliferation of DeLorean fan websites on the Internet suggests this isn't spin, though few commentators could resist recalling how notoriously poorly the low-horsepower original had performed for a roadster-class vehicle. It can hardly be coincidental that the original target audience of *Back to the Future* is now collectively cruising into middle age. What they will be buying isn't just a car, but the realisation of some kind of carbon-datable, collective cultural fantasy: a weird species of nostalgia for a fiction. Fictions are potent things.

This association of vehicle and film is the one that virtually everybody makes first, but there's also a panoramic back-story to consider. This is confirmed – to the extent that such a slippery endeavour can be said to confirm anything – by Duncan Campbell's *Make it new John* (2009), a film that traces the rise and fall of DeLorean, man and car. Its fifty minutes of archive material and self-shot footage refract the messy, paradoxical, couldn't-make-it-up tale of a Shakespearean character who lived an outsize life, the Detroit-born son of a Romanian immigrant who became a wunderkind engineer at General Motors and who, through projects like the Pontiac GTO, reshaped American idealism (the pioneer spirit, mobility as birthright) as it is incarnated in cars. It is also, to some degree, a partial window on an American Icarus who was also a Lazarus – a maverick who believed his own myth, fell to Earth and was born again at Universal Studios.

In Campbell's chronologically arranged daisy chain of various types of documentary (and non-documentary) footage, we begin with an uneasy, monochrome, borderline-cliché evocation of childhood and adolescence as demanding escape into imagination: at one point, a space-age vehicle draws itself onto paper. Then DeLorean starts work at GM, and the milieu changes to an America remade in the muscle-car mould, a sunlit arcadia of surf and girls and the Beach Boys and infinite resources. We see the screen go black following the oil crisis of the mid-'70s, and first hear DeLorean speak. (Indeed, the idea of motoring on, ethically, in a world of finite resources was key to the prescient marketing campaign he launched for his own car, which was aimed at a generation who'd seen 60s ideals run aground.) We see DeLorean go solo and decide to site his DMC factory in Northern Ireland: the shared language was tempting, the government were keen and the British Labour government, desperate to stop unemployment creating waves of Republican radicals, were keener still and underwrote the deal.

The narrative moves forward, downhill. We see DMC12 crash tests and hear vox pops and sense that not everybody likes or understands this futuristic car. We see the ideal of a workplace in which both Protestants and Catholics are employed, and DeLorean asking the government for more money and negotiating with investment bankers. We see the newly elected Conservatives nix the underwriting deal as a madcap scheme, the car performing badly in the US, Irish jobs threatened, the company's credibility undermined, redundancies, American investors withdrawing, rows of static cars on the factory floor. We hear people talking ruefully of John DeLorean's 'Concorde and Claridges' lifestyle and ask whether it's wise to keep giving him money.

And, finally, we see a handful of DeLorean workers on a sit-in in the Dunmurry factory, seemingly talking to a journalist. One by one, on various pretexts, they leave, until only one remains. His name is John, and his identity (and, of course, his livelihood) is bound up with his work. As per the film's title, then, this is seemingly the story of two Johns swept up by the winds of history and dumped on separate shores. We do not see events occurring after this, such as John DeLorean being arrested for narcotics trafficking following one last, desperate attempt to finance his company. We do not see Michael J. Fox piloting a DeLorean improbably through time and space. The story ends in Ireland, in '82, in turmoil.

But what kind of story has it been? A good proportion of the black-and-white footage that Campbell collages together is not verité, coming as it does from an era when reconstruction was the norm, rather than the exception. (Indeed, this is increasingly the case again today, in our 'docutainment' moment, leaving the era of authenticity as a strange interregnum.) Actual documentary footage really enters the mix in the DMC era. And the end of the film, at the sit-in, is aesthetically consistent but, despite its immaculately faded looks, evidently in a different register altogether: scripted by Campbell, it's a piece of existential theatre with overt, stage-managed dramatic exits and metaphoric dialogue. Now, the earlier slew of film has run through a diversity of critical angles on DeLorean – he's a marketing and engineering genius, he's a master manipulator of industrial bodies, he's self-deluded and self-interested – in a diversity of formats which have a variable relationship to biographical fact. The ending, though obviously imagined, might under such auspices be seen as more reflective and more 'true', representing the hard, unlovely economic reality that is the upshot of the economic model unpacked before.

Rather than a conclusion, however, it feels more like another unravelling. It rehearses the dubious 'human interest' model that documentaries love, and is as much a manipulation as the rest. (The conflation of the two struggling 'Johns' feels like a red herring too.) If the film has a conclusion, it's that historical fact is elusive, and if it can be apprehended at all, it won't be in the span of a short documentary. The DeLorean story sits within, and is shaped by, a swirl of geopolitical crosswinds – from the Troubles to the Yom Kippur War and the oil crisis, from the morphing political climate in the UK to the persistence of the American Dream – with a man at its centre who, obviously charismatic but apparently also very shy, can't be wholly known. The DMC12 story intersects temptingly with the present, too, in unquantifiable ways: the story of a collapsing car company chimes with the recent meltdown of the car industry in the US, for instance. These are avenues for speculative thought but they remain just that, seedbeds for argument. Indeed, seeing the past through the prism of the present might only warp it further. But in our moment, the past is never allowed to be just the past.

If the final segment of *Make it new John* has a Beckettian tenor, it's consistent with an artistic practice that has frequently questioned how we're compelled to try and come to terms with the past, and where originating meaning lies. It accordingly recalls the indelible and vertiginous line in Samuel Beckett's *Murphy*: 'In the beginning was the pun.' In Campbell's film *Falls Burns Malone Fiddles* (2003, its title incidentally referencing another Beckett character while quoting graffiti about a comfortable Nationalist area of Belfast, where Catholics were thought indifferent to sectarian violence), an agitated monologue by the actor Ewen Bremner is laid over photographic stills and film footage of West Belfast youths in the 1970s and 80s, culled from the archives of community photography organisations. The problem Bremner's disembodied character faces, loops around and articulates is that of epistemology as it relates to the archive, to true knowledge of what vanishes in the face of subjectivity. Seeking linguistic formulations that will objectively describe images of youths, or of a blistered ceiling in a burned-out room, or what sounds like a bottle being kicked over, he tries metaphoric or scientific readings (here, the imagery becomes festooned with diagrams) but repeatedly forces himself to trash his conclusions and return to first principles. That he is observing "mutations in the field of light" is about as definite as our frustrated, baffled, integrity-riddled narrator can be. You can assume that he's not about to start making television documentaries.

O Joan, no... (2006) seemingly takes *Falls Burns'* tense negotiations, its play of light and invasive sound, and plunges them into claustrophobic abstraction, a disturbing call-and-response which treats understanding as a ceaseless fumbling in blackness. For fourteen minutes, clangourous abstract and referential sounds, fleeting peripheral images, and intermittent shafts of varicoloured light from diverse sources – e.g. street lamps, rave-style glowsticks and theatrical spotlights – elicit preverbal responses. The female narrator, seemingly charged with responding to what comes at her (as Bremner's character seems to be, as we all are in our ways) gives out sighs, gulps, exhalations, sniggers, vowels, consonants and whistles, whimpering and screams. At certain points, she says what sounds like 'where' and 'when'. The film ends with a dog barking distantly in the darkness. It doesn't 'conclude'. Pointedly, none of Campbell's films really do.

They are works in which action takes place on the periphery, whether the edge of a partly known historical story (as with John DeLorean), the edge of landscape – as in the film of underpasses and roadside rubbish that he contributed to Luke Fowler's music-video compilation *Shadazz 4: Evil Eye is Source* (2002) – or, in theoretic terms, the edge of knowledge, articulation, consciousness. These peripheries are, perhaps, all equally symbolic, and are worryingly endless: not least because we live in an age of retrospection, and our culture's image banks grow every day. Make DeLorean the centre of your story and you might keep gliding outward into the wider context forever, into the indefinite blackness of archival space, with its snares of fiction – making your comprehension of whatever narrative you're trying to articulate ever harder, or making it ever clearer that the story you're telling is only one in an interconnected network of remembrances. (A cosmic analogy here would be with contemporary conceptions of the universe, in which everything and nothing is at its centre; alternatively, we could call this a rhizomatic model of narrative.)

Bernadette (2008) might be considered a kind of loose precursor to *Make it new John*. Its subject is Bernadette Devlin, the Northern Irish Socialist Republican activist who, in 1969, aged twenty-one, became the youngest woman ever elected to the British parliament. The rent strikes she organised in Derry, and the 'Battle of the Bogside' between local citizens and the Royal Ulster Constabulary that ensued, are historically considered the beginning of the Troubles. The film moves chronologically through Devlin's political career, up to a 1970s interview after she left parliament, but it's hardly a straightforward narrative. It announces itself as a construct immediately, beginning with almost forensic, clue-seeking camera movements over floors and walls, then suturing fictional monochrome footage of someone sitting in a chair with verité footage of Devlin listening. The central part of *Bernadette* is a patchwork of documentary, but the whole thirty-seven-minute film is enacted at a kind of remove: at the same time as it recounts, it performs the idea of trying to understand the meaning of a life – and a time – based on existent materials relating to it.

So we are reading in the dark. It's hard to trust what we're seeing – at one point, for instance, an interviewer either pre- or post-records his questions for Devlin – and the assembled footage is hardly conclusive. Her six-month prison term is elided; so is the Bloody Sunday massacre, which Devlin witnessed. We see demonstrators and hear a ticking clock, and the next stretch of footage features Devlin being interviewed after punching Reginald Maudling, the British Secretary of State, after he stated that the British army had shot twenty-seven civil rights protestors, and killed fourteen, in self-defence. Throughout, meanwhile, Devlin's growing personal charisma and strident eloquence – and, at times, her gauche humanity – is at once captivating and distracting: magnetic personalities shape events, we're reminded, but they also tilt our readings of history.

Again, as with *Make it new John*, this film ends with an illusory coda that is not a completing. A couple of lines from Devlin's autobiography, in voiceover, segue cleanly into a rather different first-person monologue, a simulacrum of a stream of consciousness and perhaps the sort one would have before putting pen to paper to write one's own life, in which 'Devlin' quizzes herself about the formation of her sense of self, and her relationship with her mother. If she can't wholly know herself – as nobody truly can, and first-person testimonies, too, are hardly above suspicion – what hope do we have of knowing her in thirty-seven invariably slantwise minutes? Imagery fades out here. The screen is washed out, and perhaps we're looking at overcast sky (birds appear at one point) but possibly there's no imagery at all. Flickers of animation, abstract lines, pop up occasionally, like the random flashes in *O Joan, no...*, and the monologue goes on. The cadences are familiar, their pauses and rapid gushes of phrase and irritable, conscientious reversals familiar from *Falls Burns Malone Fiddles*. It is Campbell's voice and mindset, or even a knowing adoption of an authorial persona – an idiosyncratic filter (or a modelling of it) through which all the information he purveys flows and is reshaped. The last lines of *Bernadette*, then, are spoken by an actress performing a ventriloquist monologue, written by a man seeking to locate (or really deny) the objective meaning of events occurring before his birth, with the conclusions he discovered – if any – distorted by being pushed through the scrim of media. The last lines we hear 'Bernadette' speak are these: "A voice, not your own. You don't know." It never really is, and we never truly do.

MARTIN HERBERT

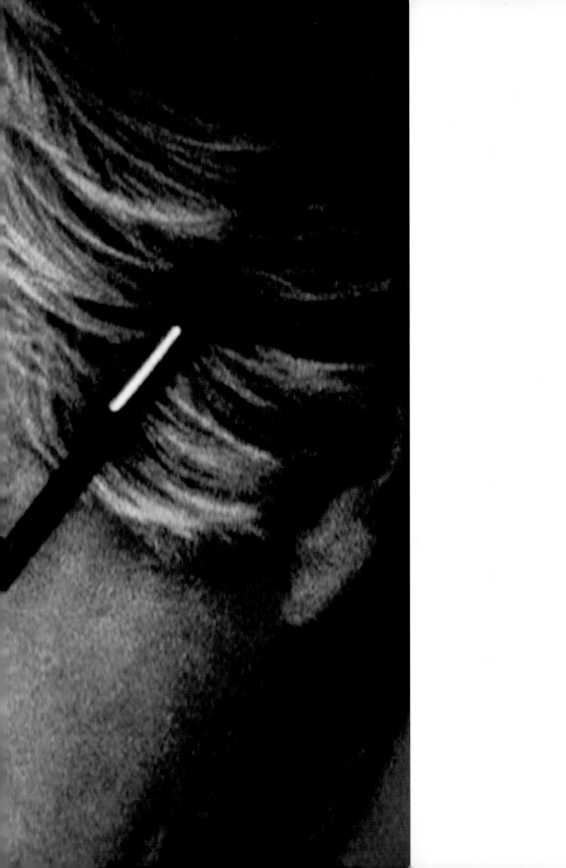

Live the

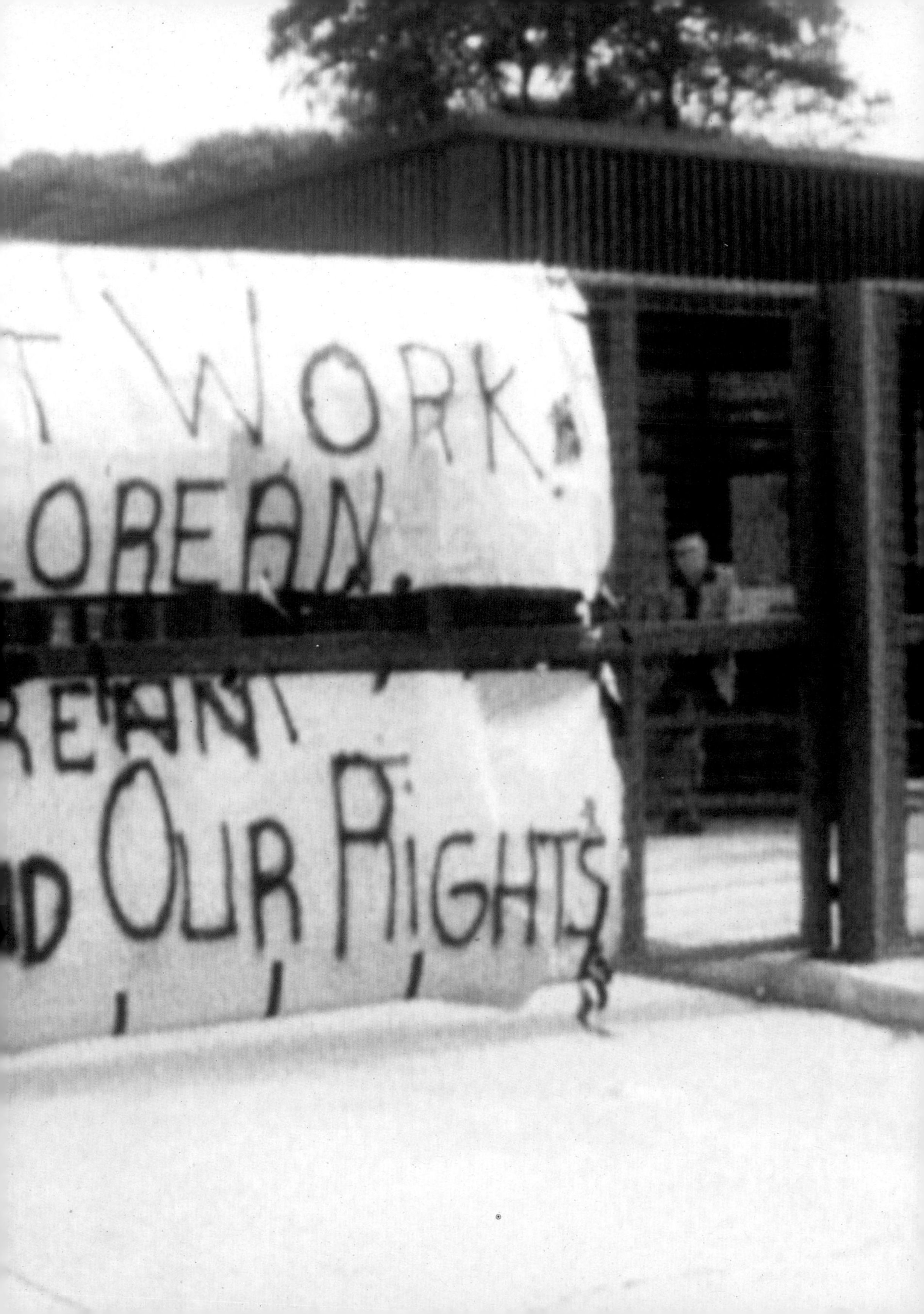
WORK
OUR RIGHTS

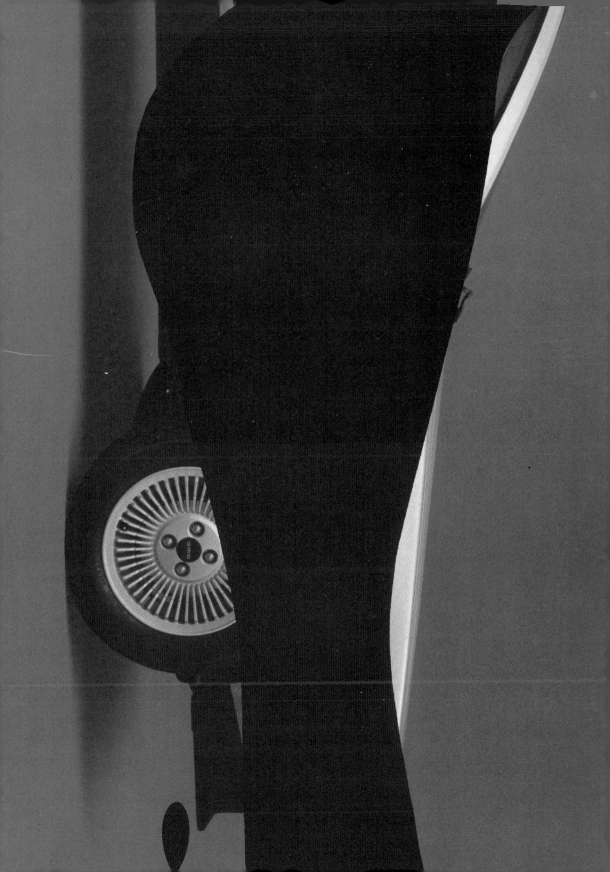

DUNCAN CAMPBELL
IN CONVERSATION WITH
MELISSA GRONLUND

**Adapted and extended from a talk
between the artist and the writer and
critic Melissa Gronlund that took place
at Chisenhale Gallery, London on 13
December 2009.**

MELISSA GRONLUND: *Your work, Duncan,
seems to me to deal with two key factors: the
archival material, or found footage of which
it is created, and the way this material is
organised. I thought I might start out by
saying a few things not about the material
but this organisation, or the representations of
different kinds of history the film moves through
– or even more specifically, different kinds
of historiography. In a book on the writing
of history* [The Analytical Philosophy of
History, 1965], *the American philosopher
Arthur Danto posits something called an 'ideal*

chronicler'; that is, someone who can both 'see' everything that it is going on in the world at one time, and who could also – simultaneously – record it. This idea of historiography is one that goes back to Leopold van Ranke, the founder of the modern discipline, who held that to write history properly one had to simply 'write it exactly as it was' – an ideal of direct recording in the writing of history that was to become possible with the film camera or video recorder, which is indeed what Danto puts forward as this 'ideal chronicler'.

As soon as he says this, however, Danto shows how the ideal chronicler as an agent of historiography is an impossibility. This is because the chronicler is only able to record; he or she is not able to synthesise, and thereby to represent history in any way that is apprehensible to the future human subject. (You can also think of Hollis Frampton's parable here, of the man who mandates in his will that his beneficiary must watch his life, recorded on film, from beginning to end, non-stop throughout his own life.) How this seems pertinent to your films is that I see them taking this question of the writing of history as central – and also of its sensibility to the present – and particularly in its often excessive use of footage the idea that too many images of the past overwhelms our ability to make sense of it.

Moreover, in Make it new John, I see four separate sections that all seem to move through some kind of conventional representation of history, often in line with the period they show – so that the subject seems less the history of DeLorean or the American love affair with the car, but the representations of this love affair. In the beginning part I can't help seeing allusions

to the early American avant-garde – Kenneth
Anger and the Surrealist-inspired plays with
reality enabled by the use of the camera – and
in the second part I see a stylised documentary
that works hard to communicate this idea of
America as young and going somewhere, in
more than one sense of the word. The third part,
which seems the bulk of the film, refers to direct
cinema or vérité documentary, and finally at
the end we have the almost quite surprising
pastiche of a BBC re-enactment, perhaps, or
more simply the idea of 'retrospection' put
directly on show. I don't know if that's too
schematic, and if that idea of a move through
genres of picturing the past is too reductive, but
I thought we could lead off with this idea of
representation.

DUNCAN CAMPBELL: You're right: the
film is quite segmented. The sections are
quite distinct and in certain cases there
are periods of black between them. This
was a response to the archival material as
I found it – rather than being intentional
from the beginning – a consequence of
dealing with a story that evolves over
several decades. The manner of
representation changes over the period of
time I was looking at. You have the type
we're most familiar with – vérité or direct
presentation. But if you look at what
precedes this – footage from the 1940s or
1950s, say – it is much more staged. In
many cases the filmmaker has used
actors rather than people on the spot.
This became part of the work. I decided
early on that I wouldn't try to homogenise
the different styles in any way: that I
would leave in the paradoxes that moving
from one section to another creates.

This interest in the different styles of representation, is that something that grew out of your previous film Bernadette, or has this been present in your work for a long time?

The period of time *Bernadette* deals with, roughly from 1969 to 1974, is quite short in relation to *Make it new John*, so there is far more continuity in the type of archival material available. It's pretty much all direct or vérité in its style. Initially I was interested in the internal tension in this style rather than the tensions between contrasting styles. I was also interested in my own part in all of this – the idea of representing a person using the scattered, mediated fragments at my disposal. There were exceptions, of course – films such as *People of Ireland* (1970) about Free Derry by Cinema Action that looked at the way events were framed by the media. It is both subjective and explicitly activist. This film, in particular, did influence the final section of *Bernadette* but still this section is more of an aposiopesis rather than a jump from one style to another. The structure of *Make it new John* and *Bernadette* are similar to the extent that they attempt to make this sort of paradox explicit.

What's also interesting about this idea of preserving, to some extent, the representative style that's contemporaneous with the material that's being shown – it also brings up another key facet of your films: that is, how we expect to see the past represented in particular ways.

Yes, this is a thread that runs through both films. They are both an attempt to understand the past, to understand it by understanding how it is rehearsed and how the present bears on this reconstructed past. Because they are fixed as a collection of representations my aim is to open up these histories rather than reveal their truth. However, with *Bernadette, Make it new John*, and also *Falls Burns Malone Fiddles*, I am interested in the specific histories that they deal with. They're very important in their own right, and I feel a responsibility towards them as such. I'm not simply using them as a device to state that historical meaning is contested, there is a balance to be had. I think that documentary relies on shorthand and parable as much as any work of fiction. So, for example, there is an obsession with subjective violence as opposed to structural or institutional violence, even with the most progressive, activist films. I recognise the limitations of this approach. With *Make it new John* I made some effort to move it away from a single figure – John DeLorean. My starting point was the car, and how it has become mythologised, but he is inextricably bound up in mythology, he is the source of much of it. So he became difficult to ignore. As well as this, his life story is epic, almost Shakespearean.

What about the politics and your interest in their relationship to Belfast? Is that political content something that motivated you, or something more personal?

It varies. With Bernadette Devlin – or McAliskey, as she is now known – she is somebody that I greatly admire. In terms of Northern Ireland she exploded a lot of the mythology and vested interest inherent in sectarian politics. I'm not so sure how present that is in the film. I used what was available from various archives but you see the media at the time didn't take her very seriously. She was this plucky girl, and that's as much they'd allow her. If anything, the film is a portrait of this parallel Bernadette Devlin and how she was variously misconstrued as a result of her iconic status.

The politics in *Make it new John* are different. They have much more to do with industrial decline in Northern Ireland and elsewhere in Britain in the 1970s and the decimation that took place once Margaret Thatcher took office. In terms of the final section of the film, which is the part that I re-enacted, one of the things that I found very hard to figure out is how uncritical DeLorean workers were of John DeLorean once the factory closed. All their ire was directed towards Margaret Thatcher and her government.

Now, or at the time? Have they changed their views?

Actually, both at the time and since. I'm generalising of course, but my impression is that the majority attitude was that if John DeLorean had been given a little bit more money, the factory would still be going. That glosses over so much. The fact is that he used large amounts of taxpayers' money to pay for things that were nothing to do with jobs in Belfast – devising a plan to take over Chrysler, paying the wages of the manager on his avocado ranch, on a snow plough company, etc. Also there are millions of pounds that went missing and have never been properly accounted for. A large part of the problem came down to the fact the original agreement to fund the project signed by Roy Mason, the Labour Secretary of State for Northern Ireland, meant that the British Government provided the majority of the capital for the project but had no effective control. I also find it difficult to ignore the fact that the DMC12 car wasn't selling at anywhere near the numbers that the plant was set up to.

DeLorean's embezzlement – you left that out of the film, didn't you? I think it's alluded to by a character but of course there is no narrator who could ground that assertion.

It's mainly to do with the period of time the film deals with, or the point at which it ends. The scene at the end was set during the sit-in, which took place during the summer of 1982. At that stage there was a faint glimmer of hope that a buyer might be found for the plant and that production might be kept going on a reduced scale. The sit-in was really an attempt by the workers to stop the government receiver, Sir Kenneth Cork, stripping the company's assets. There had been some allegations before that – DeLorean's personal secretary Marian Gibson handed over copies of his memos to a Tory MP called Nicholas Winterton. The most serious allegation to come out of these memos was that

DeLorean had lied about the amount
that he had personally invested in setting
up the company. There was a cursory
investigation but he was cleared. It wasn't
until after DeLorean was arrested for
cocaine trafficking in October 1982 that
the allegations really started flying.

*There is that hilarious moment in the film
where the wife of the – what is he? – the Lord
Mayor complains about where the gear stick is
positioned.*

That's Humphrey Atkins, the Secretary of
State for Northern Ireland and his wife.
Because of direct rule the place was in
the hands of these plummy public school
types. His wife is absolutely priceless, to
the manor born.

*One thing that your films do very well is to
qualify the notion of a history that is near
enough to still be remembered first-hand
– which can be a self-aggrandising, MTV
manoeuvre, taking cult pop artifacts as history,
and ratifying people's memories by bringing
them to the status of a more universal history.
(What made me think of this is the DeLorean
car in Back to the Future.) But in your
work, perhaps because of the exclusive and
uneditorialised use of found footage, there is
often something shaming or embarrassing
about watching it – the inexactitude of what we
remember, or how much we just don't.*

What I do is always a response to the
material. Although I might have, for
example, with *Bernadette* or *Make It New
John*, a chronology I'm trying to be
faithful to, I watch everything I can before

I decide what material to use. There are things like that clip you mentioned, of Humphrey Atkins's wife complaining about the gear stick, you could never anticipate till you've seen it. It's revealing in a way that someone speaking into a microphone on something they've thought about and prepared just isn't. Particularly in the context of a Secretary of State for Northern Ireland, who has to be incredibly careful what they say. I always try to be open for them – there are a lot in *Bernadette* as well – those unguarded moments.

Something you seem to address head-on in Bernadette, and in Make it new John as well, is a certain pleasure factor that comes from watching representations of someone else or of found footage. In Bernadette it seemed you were looking at the seductiveness of found material – embodied in this young, female figure of Bernadette – whereas with Make it new John, with the last scene, you seem to be questioning that seduction. I was struck by people's reactions to that part of the film – perhaps people felt jolted out of the lull of rehearsed images, and thrown into a situation where their critical judgement was suddenly being called for.

Yes, as I was saying earlier in the case of *Bernadette* you're really talking about a parallel Bernadette Devlin. There are elements of the film that jar, that disrupt the pleasure that comes from watching representations of her. But I'm not trying to jolt people, to say, actually, all that stuff about this fire-brand girl is rubbish, that beneath all this mystification the truth is that she was a person who could transcend sectarian attachment and class attachment, who carried a genuine mandate for popular revolution. Because this is yet another reduction or representation, a eulogy for someone still very much alive.

They're both outsider figures – Bernadette because she's young, she's a woman, DeLorean because he's an American in Northern Ireland – but you're also coming form the position of an artist-filmmaker. That's a unique place that you co-opt for yourself, and one that doesn't put you under any obligation to tell the whole story, to say, for instance, that DeLorean was arrested for cocaine consumption or procurement. The assumption is that the story already exists out there, and you're only giving a take on it.

To be not comprehensive is what I aspire to. When I was at the early stages of making *Make it new John* I was told that there were a number of Hollywood studios that have productions in the pipeline of the story of John DeLorean. You can call me a cynic, but I can imagine the story they will tell – that his arrest for drug trafficking and the protracted trial will feature quite prominently. Maybe him finding God will provide a twist of redemption at the end. If you take the period of the 70s and early 80s, that I have dealt with in the film, his lifestyle was as glamorous as it got – his wife Christina Ferrare, his friendship with Bob Hope, who invested $500,000 in his company. I decided to focus more on the economics of the DeLorean phenomenon, the desire he created for the car. It's a huge story that transcends the Troubles, and the Reagan and Thatcher new economic order. The reverberations are potentially endless. Practically speaking there are so many threads to the story anyway that you have to narrow it down.

Also those Hollywood films – Scarface, Blow – do of course take the easily moralised tone of a rise and fall, which presupposes one figure who traces that arc. Make it new John, on the other hand, seems concerned with how to represent the mass – even the ambiguity of the title, which can refer to John DeLorean or to the factory worker called John at the end, moves away from this idea of a sole protagonist. How much has this idea of trying to represent the 'many' rather than the 'one' been important to you? Some of the established cinematic ways of representing the 'mass' – vox pops, Brechtian symbolisation – that you see, for example, in critical film-making seem to be tested out, and even discarded by your film.

I think that even with the endless vox pops, which allow a direct voice, there is an idea of one body – 'The People' or 'The Workers'. There is an assumed unity. In the case of the DeLorean situation one thing that became apparent to me through reading or watching interviews with DeLorean workers is that, even within trade union organisations, not everyone was in agreement over the analysis of the situation, over what action could be taken and what they hoped to achieve by that action. This makes any easy assertion of 'the many equals the one' difficult. So the final scene of the film contains much tension, between the interviewer and the workers and between the workers themselves. It's a dysfunctional version of the idealised depictions of the masses you describe.

If we can, let's speak a bit about the final scene, which seems to loom large in people's minds. For my own part, it went from being something I was puzzled by to something that I really think is the meat of the film. Could you talk about how you wrote the script and the transition from found footage to this woman and her focus on feelings, on how the workers feel about the situation? Again, following my schemata, this shift to an individualised audience reaction serving as the representation of a given historical reality.

When I got into the research for *Make it new John* I was surprised at how un-critical the DeLorean workers were of John DeLorean after the plant closed. It wasn't just the allegations of fraud that they seemed willing to overlook but also the fact that he had used them as a political football. In a way this is understandable – their thinking is based on certain solidarities and opposition to Thatcher's government. But nevertheless it is a position that is steeped in mythology. Also practically, in terms of representing this position, their views were under-represented in the archival footage. It was far easier to get hold of printed material that related to this.

This type of re-enactment is not without precedent in documentary film. In fact I would say that it is becoming far more common. I had anticipated that the

transition from the archival to the re-
staged would be a jolt but essentially I see
them as no different.

I have been surprised that some people
have interpreted this section as a
sentimental attempt to personalise and
counterpoint the mediated notion of
history contained in the archival footage
that precedes it. This is very far from
what I intended. I do not think that this
section of the film to be any closer to the
'truth' or carrying any greater revelation
than any other part. It does not purport
to be authentic – in fact it is as explicitly
manipulated as the rest.

Inexplicably someone is removed from
the shot; then they leave one by one. At
the end you are left with the solitary figure
of John. The tone of the interview shifts
decisively from the social to the private.
John resists the interviewer's questions
but is eventually harassed into giving
up some personal information. Then it
abruptly ends.

Or you could say it unravels. As far as I'm
concerned nothing is resolved or revealed
by this. The story, the history to which it
refers is left open.

*How does this relate to your earlier works – for
example, could you explain more about a film
like* O Joan, no... [2006], *which is much
more formal, and relates to this idea of the
representational?*

The primary elements of O Joan, no...
are the black screen and silent narrator.

The black screen is interrupted by a series of random lights – streetlights, theatre lights, glow sticks, etc – which provokes a response from the narrator. There is no narrative or pattern to these responses. The voice is perplexed, annoyed, amused, exasperated, at various turns. I'm aware, when watching a film, that I have a tendency to perceive a narrative even where there is none. I was very interested in making the relationship between what happens on the screen and the narrator's voice a tense one. The idea was that the two would be at odds as opposed to their usual passive/complementary relationship. Although this film is formal in terms of its lack of an obvious social or political context – it is not 'about' anything as such – there is an element of this tense relationship between narrator/image in most of my films.

There's seems to be a quite clear dialectical relationship that was also present in the black and white and the sound and silence – it comes like a burst onto the screen and then you are left wondering what happens, and then you have to watch it a few times before you realise the question of what happens is the question that runs all the way through.

It's the one film I've made which is consciously made with this idea of it being an ambient work – it was made for a space where people are not provided with timings, it was shown on a loop and it was difficult to tell where it began and ended. With the other films I have made I have a preference for people sitting down and watching them from beginning to end and so always try to provide times.

Do you want to talk a little here about the sculpture you used at Tramway?

The idea that I had first had for Tramway was for a much larger structure – a wall made of a two-way mirror. In the end it proved too expensive. What I ended up using were four pyramids with an open base that were mirrored on the inside. In a well-lit space, because of the way the mirror recedes, you can always see your own reflection in these as you move through the space. With the space blacked they rely on the light from the screen to activate them so the effect is intermittent. The space just below the ceiling at Tramway is quite busy with lots of lighting, heating and other fixtures. The idea was that they would take their place amongst all of this.

Were you trying to instil self-consciousness in the viewers while watching the film?

That was the idea at the beginning but in the end I think it was far more about creating a consciousness of the space. This is something that has been on my mind a lot recently. What does it mean to show a film like the one I have made in a gallery space? Is it simply a de facto cinema or do the screen and all the other apparatus become sculptural objects because they happen to be in such a space? How does it relate to a tradition of expanded ambient film? And so on …

There was a recent conference in London on expanded cinema that was subtitled 'activating the space of reception' – that does sound like a slogan – which might relate back to the idea we spoke of before about reception being as important as representation.

Yes, but the space of reception is not something I feel I can fully exert myself over. To be honest a large part of the reason I show these films in galleries is quite mundane – it boils down to practicality of where I can get the money to produce them in the first place. I do feel that *Bernadette* and *Make it New John* in particular fall between two stools. In the talk we took part in at Chisenhale someone made the point that this tension was useful, that it was potentially productive. I agree, but somehow I would like it to be more consciously unresolved.

I think that might be a nice place to end it – this idea of 'conscious unresolution', which is, as well, how Make it new John itself ends.

MELISSA GRONLUND is a critic based in London, and Managing Editor of *Afterall* and *Afterall Online*. She is also a visiting tutor at the Ruskin School of Drawing and Fine Art, University of Oxford.

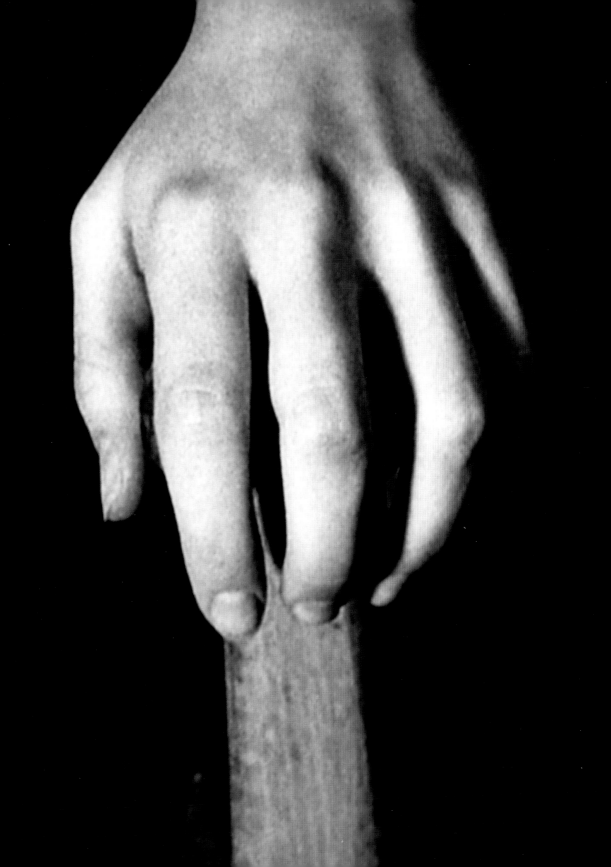

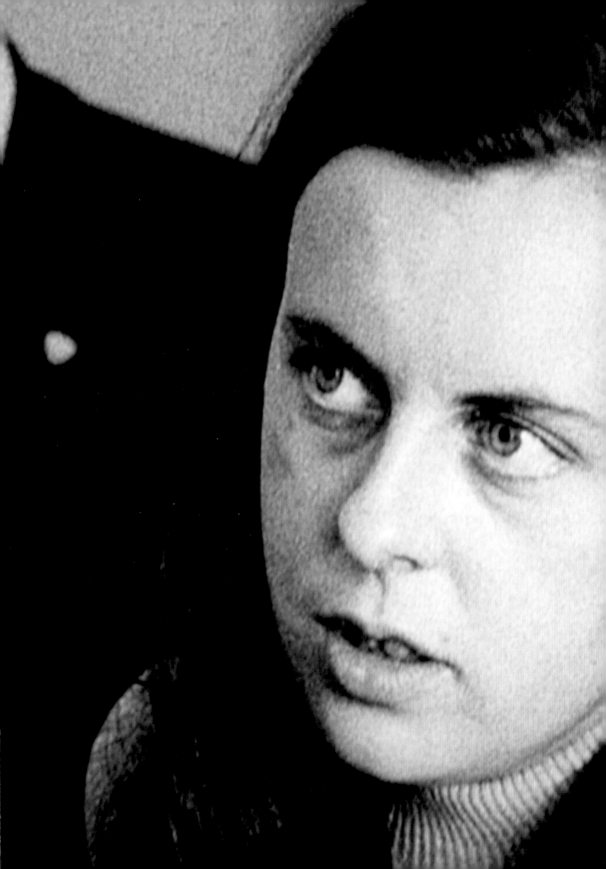

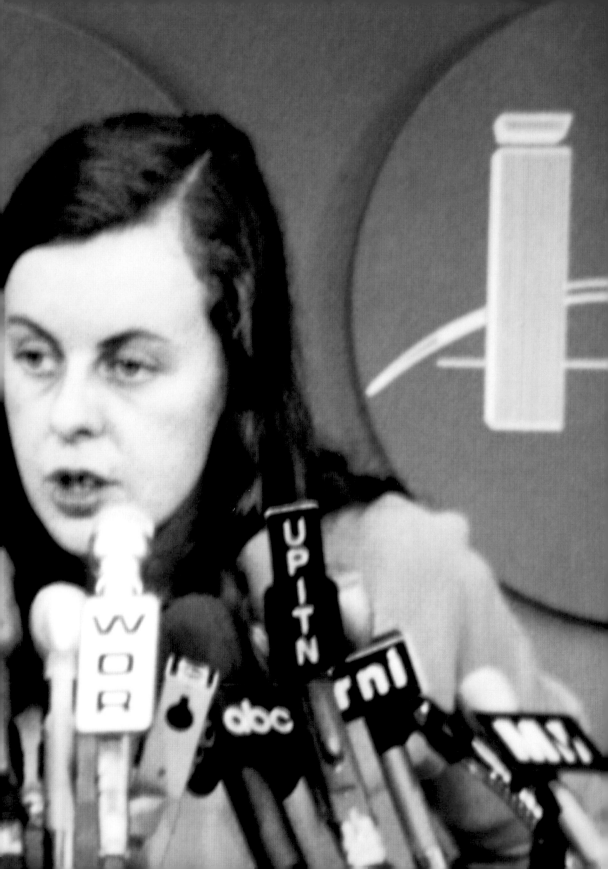

CLASS & SUBCULTURES: A VERSION OF COHEN'S MODEL

DETERMINATE
CONDITIONS

WORKING CLASS RESPONSES

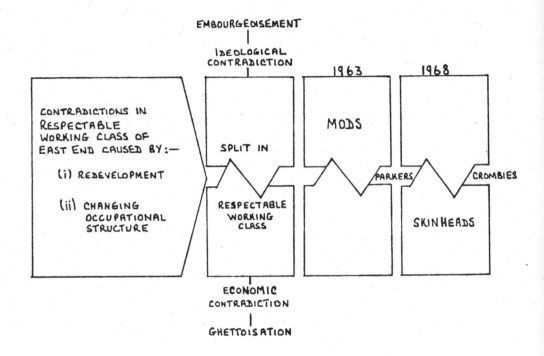

'Alone again'

Image changes.

'How does it feel.

Image changes.

When the musics over.'

Image changes.

'Is this where it is.'

Image changes.

'Find it again.'

Image changes.

'Shades of rhythm'

Oh to hell with this. My impressions disgust me. To hell with their appearing, me considering, me hailing, their turning, my saying - 'this thing is worthy of an caption', me commending, their intoning. It has nothing to do with my impressions. I made the mistake of being, of trying to be through them, of allowing them to move me to make the statements I have. If only I could remove my own being from the discussion. If I did that there would be no discussion, nothing. Well perhaps not nothing. Something resembling nothing, but not nothing. But let us suppose for a moment that I was, lets be kind, simply deluded, about my part in all this. Then the attribution of certain qualities - bodies even - to elements within the figures or pictures or lights might not be totally erroneous. It all amounts to a case of mistaken identity - it is not about I but about they - a basic error really. It is they who have lives, adversaries, mind, senses. Its possible, at least as possible as my own possession of such like.

Footage of Divis Flats.

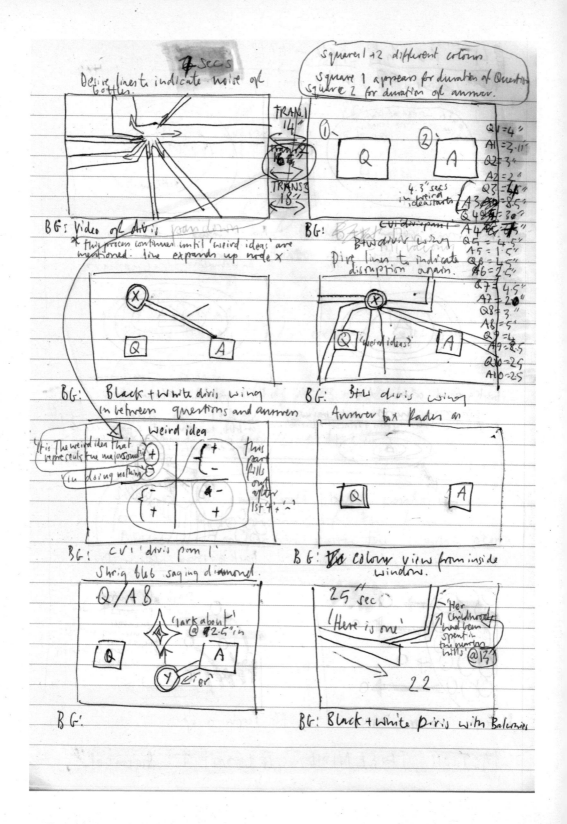

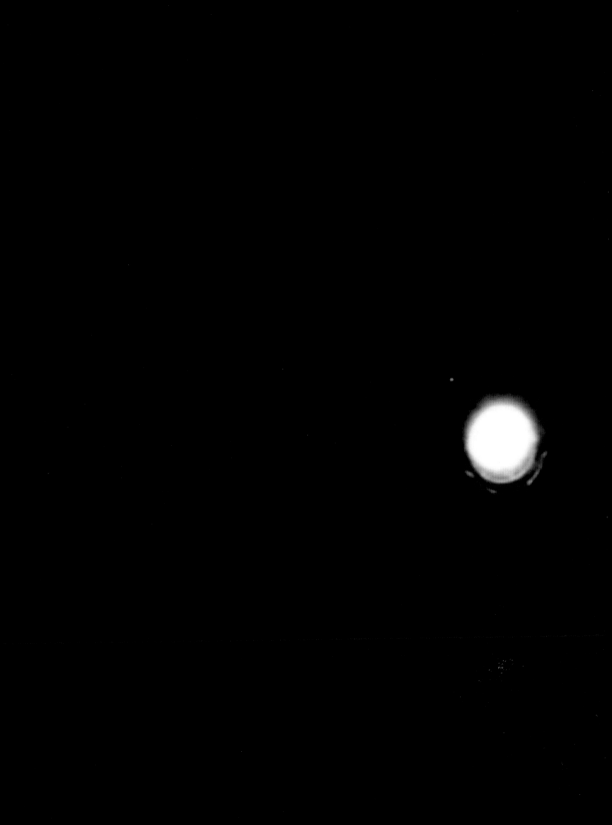

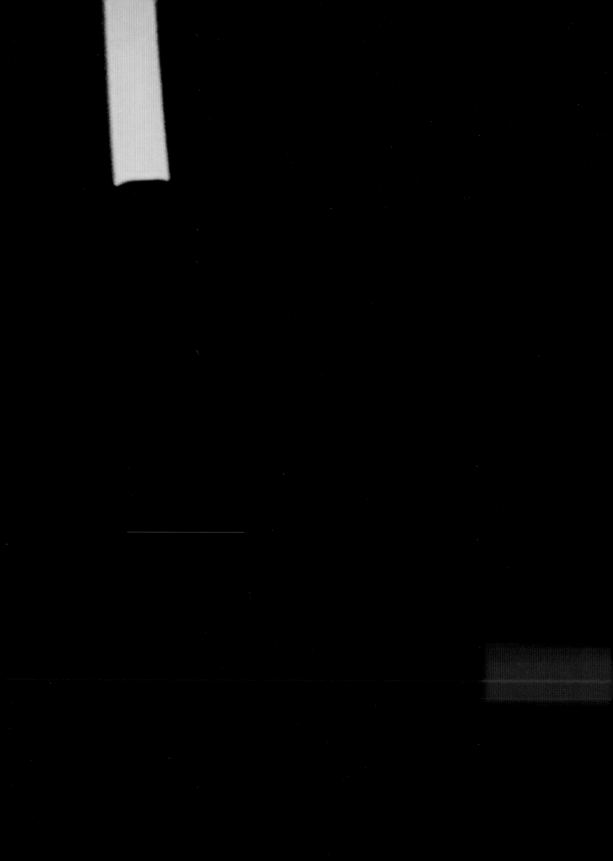

DUNCAN CAMPBELL

Born Dublin, Ireland, 20 July 1972

Lives and works in Glasgow

EDUCATION

1996-8 MFA, Glasgow School of Art

1993-6 BA, University of Ulster at Belfast

1992 National College of Art and Design, Dublin

SELECTED SOLO EXHIBITIONS

2010

The Model, Sligo

Artists Space, New York

Tramway, Glasgow

2009

Chisenhale Gallery, London

Museum Moderner Kunst Stiftung, Vienna

Bernadette, MIT, Boston

Duncan Campbell, Ludlow 38, New York

Duncan Campbell, Kunstverein Munich

Bernadette, Scottish National Gallery of Modern Art

2008/09

Bernadette, HOTEL, London

Duncan Campbell, Baltic, Gateshead

2008

0-60, ICA, London

Art Statements, Art Basel 38, Solo presentation

2006

The Unnamable, Lux at Lounge, London

2005

Something in Nothing, TART Contemporary, San Francisco

2004

Falls Burns Malone Fiddles, Galerie Luis Campaña, Cologne

2003

Falls Burns Malone Fiddles, Transmission Gallery, Glasgow

SELECTED GROUP EXHIBITIONS

2009/2010

Asking Not Telling, Institute of Contemporary Art, Philadelphia

2009

Fight The Power, Museo Nacional Centro de Arte Reina Sofia

Border Crossings, Current Art and Modernism in the 21st Century, Kunstmuseum
Wolfsburg

2008

After October, Elizabeth Dee Gallery, New York

Rictus Grin, curated by Christopher Eamon and Anke Kempkes, Broadway 1602,
New York

2007

You Have Not Been Honest, Museo D'Arte Donnaregina, Naples

2006

Art Now, Tate Britain, London

Archeology of Today? The Kosova Art Gallery, Pristina

Ein Zentrum in der Peripherie, Galerie-Peripherie, Sudhaus Tübingen

2005

Art From Glasgow, Temple Bar Gallery, Dublin

Archeology of Today? Els Hanappe Underground, Athens

The Need to Document, Halle für Kunst, Lueneburg

2004

Manifesta 5, European Biennial of Contemporary Art, San Sebastian

Emotion Eins, Frankfurter Kunstverein, Frankfurt am Main

Revolution is Not What it Used to Be, S1 Artspace, Sheffield

2003

Advertence, festival of documentary film - Various venues Belfast and Dublin.

Fresh and Upcoming, project with Luke Fowler at Frankfurter Kunstverein,
Frankfurt am Main

Old Habits Die Hard, Sparwasser HQ Berlin and Norwich Gallery

2002

Avantoscope, experimental film and music festival at KIASMA, Helsinki

Flicer, De Overslag, Eindhoven

Shadazz, Royal College of Art in London

see (www.shadazz.co.uk)

SELECTED BIBLIOGRAPHY

2009

Tobias Maier, *Mousse*, Issue 18, April - May, cover and p.27-30

Jeremy Millar, 'Top Five', *Art Review*, Issue 29, January-February 2009, p.32

Mary Brodbin, 'Bernadette', *Socialist Review*, No.332, January 2009 pp. 33-34

'Review of Bernadette', *Sleek Magazine* No.21, Winter 2008/9, pp. 118

Duncan Campbell: 'Bernadette', *The Guardian Guide*, 27th Dec-2nd Jan 2009, p.33

2008

Stuart Comer, 'Best of 2008', *Artforum*, No. 4, December 2008, p. 63

'Life in Film: Duncan Campbell', *Frieze* Issue 118, October, p.54-55

Ken Neil, 'Telling Stories', *Map*, Issue 15, Autumn, pp.36-41

Martin Herbert, 'Focus: Duncan Campbell', *Frieze* 114, April 2008, p.150-151

2007

Now and Then: Art Now at Tate Britain, Lizzie Carey-Thomas, Martin Herbert, Mary Horlock, Katherine Stout, Tate Publishing

You Have Not Been Honest, Colin Ledwith and Polly Staple, British Council

O Joan, No..., Gair Boase, Tate Britain

2006

Falter, I..., Daniel Jewesbury, Lux, London

Open Frequency, Sarah Lowndes, Axisweb

2005

The Need to Document, Edited by Sabine Schasch-Cooper, Bettina Steinbrugge, JPR Ringier

2004

With All Due Intent, Marta Kuzma and Massimiliano Gioni, Manifesta Foundation catalogue

2002

Quartet, Shadazz, Evil Eye is Source, VHS publication, The Modern Institute, bdv/ Artview

SELECTED COLLECTIONS

Tate, London, UK

MIT, Boston, USA

National Galleries of Scotland, UK

MUMOK, Vienna, Austria

CREDITS

Frontispiece
Untitled
© DeLorean Motor Company
(1975-1982)

p. 11
Make it new John 2009
Screenshot
With thanks to
Pennebaker Hegedus Films

p. 12/13
Make it new John 2009
Screenshot
With thanks to
Pennebaker Hegedus Films

p. 14/15
John DeLorean (right) and
Chief Engineer Bill Collins
(holding door) review the first
completed prototype in 1977
DeLorean Motor Company
with thanks to James
Espey, Bill Collins and Jerry
Williamson

p. 16/17
Make it new John 2009
Screenshot
With thanks to
BBC Motion Gallery

p. 18/19
Make it new John 2009
Screenshot
With thanks to RTE

p. 20/21
Installation, Tramway,
Glasgow 2010
Photo: Alan Dimmick

p. 22/23
Thanks to Seamus Harahan

p. 24/25
The 'traveling roadshow' to
introduce prospective dealers
to the DeLorean car involved
the prototype and a display
engine. In all 345 dealers paid
$25,000 for the rights to sell
the DeLorean car.
DeLorean Motor Company
with thanks to James Espey,
Bill Collins and Jerry
Williamson

p. 26/27
© DeLorean Motor Company
(1975-1982)

p. 28/29
Make it new John 2009
Screenshot
With thanks to RTE

p. 30/31
Make it new John 2009
Screenshot
With thanks to RTE

p. 32/33
Make it new John 2009
Screenshot

p. 34
Make it new John 2009
Print: glicee and silk-screen
print
59.2 x 44 cm
© Duncan Campbell
Courtesy Chisenhale
Gallery, London

p. 51
Bernadette 2008
Screenshot

p. 52/53
Bernadette 2008
Screenshot
With thanks to RTE

p. 54
Bernadette 2008
Poster: silk-screen print
80 x 52 cm
© Duncan Campbell
Courtesy Hotel

p. 55
Bernadette 2008
Screenshot
With thanks to RTE

p. 56/57
Bernadette 2008
Screenshot

p. 58
Bernadette 2008
Screenshot

p. 59
*People's Democracy/ The Falls
Burns Malone Road Fiddles*
(75.5 cm x 51 cm), Silk screen
print
CAIN, Northern Ireland Social
and Political Archive

p. 60
Falls Burns Malone Fiddles 2003
Research and drawings for
animation
© Duncan Campbell

p. 61
Falls Burns Malone Fiddles 2003
Page from script
© Duncan Campbell

p. 62/63
Falls Burns Malone Fiddles 2003
Screenshot
With thanks to Belfast Exposed

p. 64
Falls Burns Malone Fiddles 2003
Research and drawings for
animation
© Duncan Campbell

p. 65
Falls Burns Malone Fiddles 2007
Poster: silk-screen print
92.7 x 62.9 cm
© Duncan Campbell
Courtesy Hotel

p. 66/67
Falls Burns Malone Fiddles 2003
Screenshot
With thanks to Community
Visual Images, Belfast

p. 68/69
Falls Burns Malone Fiddles 2003
Screenshot
With thanks to Belfast Exposed

p. 70/71
Falls Burns Malone Fiddles 2003
Screenshot
With thanks to Belfast Exposed

p. 72/73
O Joan, no... 2006
Screenshots

p. 75
Quartet 2003
Screenshot

Endpiece
Untitled
© DeLorean Motor Company
(1975-1982)

Cover
John DeLorean addresses the
media and takes questions
at the 1978 groundbreaking
for the DeLorean factory in
suburban Belfast, Northern
Ireland.
DeLorean Motor Company
with thanks to James Espey,
Bill Collins and Jerry
Williamson

· *Make it new John* 2009
16mm film transferred to
Digi-Beta
50 min
Commissioned by Film and
Video Umbrella, Chisenhale
Gallery, Tramway and The
Model, Sligo.
© Duncan Campbell
Courtesy Hotel

· *Bernadette* 2008
16mm transferred to Digi-Beta
37 minutes
© Duncan Campbell
Courtesy Hotel

· *O Joan, no...* 2006
16mm transferred to digital
video
12 minutes
© Duncan Campbell
Courtesy Hotel

· *Falls Burns Malone Fiddles* 2003
DVD
33 minutes
© Duncan Campbell
Courtesy Hotel

· *Quartet* 2003
DVD
5 minutes
© Duncan Campbell and
Mary Hill

DUNCAN CAMPBELL

Published by Film and Video Umbrella and Tramway, in association with
The Model, Sligo

Edited by Steven Bode
Designed by Secondary Modern, London
Printed by Calverts, London

Publication supported by Arts Council England and Scottish Arts Council

ISBN: 978-1-904270-32-4

Film and Video Umbrella
8, Vine Yard, London SE1 1QL
t +44 (0)20 7407 7755
e info@fvu.co.uk
www.fvu.co.uk

Tramway
25, Albert Drive, Glasgow G41 2PE
t +44 (0) 141 276 0950
e info@tramway.org
www.tramway.org

Thanks to Lorraine Wilson, Sarah Munro, Claire Jackson and Stuart Gurden at
Tramway; Mike Jones, Bevis Bowden, Brada Barassi, Annika Kristensen, Karen
Murray and Nina Ernst at Film and Video Umbrella; Polly Staple and Andrew
Bonacina at Chisenhale Gallery; Seamus Kealy at The Model, Sligo

Duncan Campbell would like to thank: Hotel
For *Quartet*: Luke Fowler; Jonnie Wilkes
For *Falls Burns Malone Fiddles*: Belfast Exposed; Community Visual Images
For *O Joan, no...*: Kelly Campbell; Lorraine Wilson; Tramway, Glasgow
For *Bernadette*: Daniel Jewesbury; Calum Pearson; Fred Pederson; Karen Vaughan
For *Make it new John*: Siofra Campbell; Robert Lamrock; Karen Vaughan

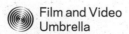